RESCUE YOUR HAPPINESS

Mara Salas

GUÍA PRÁCTICA PARA RENACER TU VIDA DESPUÉS DE UNA SEPARACIÓN

Prentice Trevenant Anant
Mara Salas

Order this book online at www.trafford.com
or email orders@trafford.com

Most Trafford titles are also available at major online book retailers.

Printed in the United States of America.

ISBN: 978-1-4269-9360-2 (sc)
ISBN: 978-1-4269-9361-9 (e)

Library of Congress Control Number: 2011915659

Trafford rev. 08/25/2011

 www.trafford.com

North America & international
toll-free: 1 888 232 4444 (USA & Canada)
phone: 250 383 6864 ♦ fax: 812 355 4082

DEDICATED TO

God, our Creator, who gave us life.

Our respective families, whose members have filled up us with an infinite love and without their constant support, we would not be what we are.

Life and all the people that we have shared, through good and bad experiences, because we have learned from all of them.

All of you, our dear readers, honestly hoping that reading this material contribute to reach your welfare and happiness.

ACKNOWLEDGEMENTS

To GOD for founding us.

To the experiences that we have lived, which have let us get through in our spiritual path and help others to keep on going.

To all of those who have accompanied us, giving us support in our every day, believing in our honest wishes.

To all the people that by letting us participate from their life experiences, with their rewarding testimonies that have contributed in an invaluable way to the elaboration of this book.

CONTENTS

PROLOGUE

"RESCUE YOUR HAPPINESS"

It *is* a practical and simple guide that has the purpose of helping you to rebuild your life after a marriage split or separation, no matter what the origin of the event was. Every time you feel unable of overcoming that relation that left footprints, that one that marked your life, obliging you to follow a pattern of victim that you do not have to play. Our goal is to assist you in regaining your inner happiness.

This is a book which will help you to raise your self esteem. It will provide you the teachings and wisdom you require to grow as an individual and to value yourself. In the same manner, it will supply you the necessary tools to avoid repeating past mistakes. As a matter of fact, one of the biggest obstacles that leads you to astray from your happiness is your own lack of love and self-esteem. Besides this, your fear to change, loneliness, and specially to have a failure. It is that fear that prevents you from fighting for your own well being, for that love that shows up with hope again and is rejected by the fear to fail once more and permitting your fears to take place instead of your hopes and in that way you forget to believe in your self, without noticing that every day that passes cannot be recovered because we live only once.

It is a guide to always take on you, is a manual that can be opened randomly and provide you with the answer you need at that precise moment.

DREAMS CAN NEVER BE BROKEN

If separation was the only pain to be felt through life, we all would be happy, because using the right tools it would be resolved; and if the breakup comes to be  qualified as a sort of "widowhood", better is to save the mourning, the flowers and the funeral expenses.

You must be objective, strong and go out like a brave blind, without an arm to lean on, without a dog or cane and tell to yourself:

"NO ONE'S WORTH MORE THAN ME"

And even the consequences of a divorce or any separation can be multiple and complicated, everything can be outstripped. There is no such thing as perfect relationships, relationships are very valuable and strong tools to evolve; we will always share our lives with the persons that give us the opportunity to learn and grow up.

The breakups are unpredictable, but needed; a "must", this is to say a "duty", something that even though we try to avoid, sometimes is needed to be lived.

Habit is sometimes stronger than love and we persist in a relationship because of the fear to be alone, to the unknown, to social pressure, amongst other causes, without thinking that a separation can bring great benefits, if you learn from the committed mistakes and you open yourself to true happiness.

It is impossible to suffer for love, we suffer due to emotional lacks, marks and wounds.

A lot of people believe that they are living a great love because they sacrifice and leave behind their activities and interests. Love is happiness, welfare; love is to live harmonically.

Suffering is not needed to be happy.

One of the most important duties that human being has is to love itself. So, even if you do not love yourself, have for granted that nobody is going to love you as deep as you wish. Remember that you have your other half or soul mate. The person you are waiting for truly exists.

Renounce to suffer, decree your happiness, give welcome to love, joy, peace, to abundance and prosperity in its widest meaning. No obstacle can get in the way, everything depends on your will.

Remember that the only thing that makes a dream impossible is the fear to failure.

 Our purpose is to help you to be happy, to get through your pain and make you stronger. Promote your growth as a being alive joy deserving person, as a worthy person of its own life. Without doubt we have the power when we are decided. Do not forget that when we really want something, there is no obstacle capable to interpose.

It is common to hear the popular saying "is better to be alone than in bad company". However, we find people that are in a completely damaged relationship and they justify hanging on because of love. This is not true. Tolerate mistreatment, aloud the insupportable, it is not love. The saddest thing about it is that a lot of people do not even ask why? The answer is fear, but that fear only responds to ego, yes, to that own ego that we maintain cheating us and keeps us away from happiness.

A lot of people do not breakup because cowardice, because of not having the courage required to stop a torture that has become a roller coaster, that causes dizziness, strong nausea and negative sensations, in the amusement park of a society in which humans seem more attached to pain than to happiness. Humans grasp to an impossible past, to habits and to inner masochism.

Denisse Troconis Aoun & Mara Salas

First of all, I propose you not to give up your dreams, always choose to be happy, use the following numerated tools and your life will truly change and you will be able to make your dreams come true. However, a lot of mental discipline that will be obtained during practice is required. Train for your most important race: "Life".

LOVE YOURSELF, ACCEPT YOURSELF, APPROVE YOURSELF, AND RESPECT YOURSELF

This is the fundamental key to achieve success in all your life areas. Approve and accept yourself now; this is the first step to a positive change in all life's areas.

KEEP ALWAYS A POSITIVE MIND, EVEN IN THE WORSE CIRCUMSTANCE, BE POSITIVE

Always seed positive thoughts in your mind and automatically negative thoughts will be reduced. Avoid every negative thing, and when I say negative I mean everything that disturbs, sadden or depress you, including people, things and activities. Find a joy potential in everything that you do, whether you are cooking, cleaning or working. Escape from negativity. You must work in your goals with the certainty that everything will turn out alright and enjoying present tense.

FOCUS ON YOUR BREATHING

With your eyes closed, breathe deep and slowly focus in the inhale and exhale acts. You will feel a pleasant relaxation and you will be filled with peace and energy. Besides, you will be purifying your body by oxygenating it. Do this several times a day.

LIVE IN THE PRESENT TENSE, IT IS THE ONLY TIME AT OUR DISPOSITION

Present tense is always the moment to act. When are changes made? The Answer: Here and Now. It does not matter for how long we have been following a negative pattern, today we can start changing. Focus on here and now and completely take pleasure from each moment. Past has been gone and future has not come yet.

PRAY, PRAYING HAS MIRACULOUS RESULTS

Always repeat "I trust in you, Jesus", and you will see great miracles.

READ SPIRITUAL GROWING BOOKS, SELF-HELP BOOKS

This sort of readings contributes you with the necessary tools to advance in your spiritual path. This kind of readings will get you closer to achieve making your dreams come true.

CLEAN YOUR MENTAL HOUSE, CLEAN YOU INNER SELF

This means to take out "your inner trash", to expulse negative thoughts from your interior, as well as sadness, rancor, hate, frustration and resentment feelings. Feelings like this are a true weight, a heavy load, and you are the most injured.

FORGET AND FORGIVE

Forgiveness is the master key to happiness. Without forgiveness there is no peace. Rancor and hate poison your soul, decrease your energy and keep you away from living a harmonic life.

CONNECT TO PEOPLE AND ACTIVITIES THAT PRODUCE YOU WELL-BEING

Tune up yourself in the channel of joy, harmony, faith, peace, hope and above all things, love. I recommend you to meet new places and new people, do not let routine to catch you, that fear impedes you to try once again. Negativity is abstract, but no one is exempt from feeling what floats in the air, the things that match, conscious or unconscious, with the spirit. Spirit can be felt, is like the very wind that can't be seen, but we all know because we breathe it and see how it moves plants, trees and waters.

CONNECT TO NATURE'S ENERGY

Walk barefoot in the sand, visit a park, mountain or beach, take a bath in the sea, a river or a waterfall, without any doubt you will refill your energy and feel renewed.

LISTEN TO MUSIC THAT MAKES YOU SING AND DANCE

The vibration of a song has the power to makes us feel alive, let emotions and feelings emerge. If you watch TV or go to the movies, try to choose comedies, musicals or documentaries avoid seeing programs or movies which content refers to calamities, disasters, dramas or tragedies.

VISUALIZE YOU LIVING THE RELATIONSHIP THAT YOU WISH

Visualization plays a vital role to achieve your success. When you watch yourself continuously possessing you goals, your unconscious mind searches the ways to make it true. Clearly and precisely visualize your objectives as often as you can, preferably when you wake up and when you go to sleep. Create a clear mental image of your objective. You must create a real image as if you have already achieved your goal and create the moment emotion in your body. You must see, listen and feel like if you have already reached your goal.

BE THANKFUL EVERY MORNING FOR BEING ALIVE AND ALL THE RECEIVED BLESSINGS

Appreciate your health, family, work and friends. There is always a lot of things to be thankful for, more than we think generally. Be thankful for your life, for who you are, for what you have. Every time you say ¡Thanks! You are generating a good thought. Thank for all things, talk about good things and be thankful for everything, even the challenges you are living, because thanks to them you can grow up and create the life you wish so much. Avoid complaining, because you will attract to you the negative charge of your words.

REPEAT THROUGH ALL DAY THOSE STATEMENTS THAT MAKE YOU FEEL WELL

Positive affirmations are positive thoughts that you choose to introduce in your conscience so in that way you produce the wished results, through repetition. Next, I give an example of them: I am love, I am successful, I am health, I am a magnet to attract perfect love to my life, I do accept and approve myself exactly as I am, my life is wonderful, wellness, prosperity and abundance flow through me, there is no negative energy that can affect me, I'm always safe and protected.

PRACTICE MEDITATION, PRACTICE YOGA

Look for a time to connect with your inner self, to calm down your mind, to relax, to be quiet and meet with yourself.

DO EXERCISE AND A HEALTHY MEAL

Take care of your body so you can enjoy an excellent life quality. Exercise release endorphins providing you with an immediate wellness. If you do not like gyms, you can walk, trot or practice any sport. "Move yourself".

LAUGH, IS ONE OF THE BEST SECRETS THAT LIFE GIVES US

Laughing is to fill up with youth and vitality. Laughter is the best plastic surgery, the best medic and the best healer. Laugh about everything.

Help yourself at first instance and if you need extra help do not hesitate to contact a psychologist, a spiritual coach or other qualified person.

LEARN TO BE PRACTICAL

Behave practically. Being practical is not to stop feeling or letting frivolity to govern you. Being practical is to be smart, to decide letting behind all the suffering and to grab the wheel of your life, setting the necessary strategies to abandon sadness and the being victimized sensation.

When someone consults me crying, regretting things "that could have been and did not happened", I simply ask them: ¿Who is dead?, and as I receive a negative answer I highlight the fact that life has not finished, and that the first step to be followed in order to recover happiness, consists in analyze our inner self and release everything that oppress us.

It is very important that you talk to yourself, or shout the thing that bother you, even you understand what these things are, in order to take out the pain from your soul, you can write and burn everything that afflicts and affects you.

Release your concerns in front of a mirror and remember that power is inside you. In a lot of cases, it is not the best option to tell your best friend, because sometimes it is not the right person.

Remember that no one loves you more than you do and also remember that envy and evil are the human rodents that eat others happiness. That is why it is important that you elevate your self-esteem and I repeat and invite you to repeat yourself as many times as it is necessary:

¡NO ONE'S WORTH MORE THAN ME!

A SUCCESSFUL BREAKUP

In order to achieve a successful breakup we must remember that: Today is the Tomorrow's Yesterday. Undoubtedly this is true, and I would like you to focus your actions in living today, here and now. Living every day at its own time.

I was not born to transmit negativity and much less to receive it, unfortunately there is a lot of people that hold on to past negative experiences. If you are one of this people hooked up in the past, I want to insist you in the fact that past is already gone and does not exist anymore, is like the spilled water that can't be gathered again. We only have the present tense. Live today, only the anxious lives the future and only the rancorous lives the past.

The worse storm in your life, the conflict, is already gone and now is your new teacher. Good news is that the pain you lived has make you grow as a human being and opens you the path to your real happiness. You must understand it so, because so it is: Leave behind your painful past right now, because from today and after a new day and a new future begins to you, a new life that transforms you and brings new opportunities to you. You can't lock up yourself in sadness, neither to fall in an insensate depression that only shows weakness, insecurity and an enormous fear before the exciting adventure that life is giving you. Every new dawn is a new opportunity.

Life gives not one but several opportunities and we simply miss them many times, when we hook up in sadness, or accepting a harmful situation. Your past and your conflicts have been left behind and you can't let them to drag yourself just like if your life would have end with your separation. You can get over a breakup or a divorce by taking conscience of what happened, learning from your mistakes and treasuring yourself as the wonderful person you are.

I recommend you to visualize a conversation with your former partner in which you say:

"I am sorry for you, but my life do not finishes because of you, on the contrary, our separation aloud me start living a better period".

SEPARATION'S IMPACT ON CHILDREN

A breakup or divorce is a painful process, specially to your children and if they are not able to get over it, this process will impact them, in many cases, on their personal development. Children, unlike adults, do not perceive divorce as a second chance, despite how old they are.

Divorce generates affection and attention hunger in children.

For human being is important to have good memories about their parent's relationship, they do need to know their parents loved each other sometime in order to confirm the good things in them and their origin.

Divorce is a different experience to parents than to children. Children loose a basic element to development: familiar structure.

For children family is the entity that provides them with the needed support and protection. Children blame their parents for have failed in one of the most important tasks in life, that is to keep united family and partnership, through richness and poorness, through happiness and misfortune.

Children's first reaction to divorce is fear due to the deep sensation of loss and sadness. Children fight against their anger feelings through years. Most of the children keep the faith in their parents to reunite, they feel lonely and helpless. A lot of children in school age present and complain about psychosomatic symptom such stomach or headache.

Children's anger is united to an impotence feeling. They feel their opinion is not considered and that they can't have influence in such a big event in their life. A lot of children feel guilty and others feel as an obligation of their own to reconstruct their parents' relationship. Conflicts about loyalty to parents appear too.

When a parent abandons the other parent, children understand this as if they were abandoned. Many teenagers are driven to identify themselves with the rejected parent due to compassion and affection. As they grow up, they fear to use the "love" word because relationships are uncertain and do not trust in commitment because their parents broke theirs. Divorce children usually postpone their own children until they are sure their relationship is working alright.

A new partner appearance in a parent's life raises conflict and uncertainty about the conduct to this new partner because to loyalty with the real father or mother.

It results hard to children to be certain about if they are betraying with their missing father or mother.

Relationship of your new partner and your children is built through countless agreements, through which your children perceive that your partner cares about them; sometimes there can appear certain identity conflicts that were missing before.

Some children can find in their stepfather or stepmother a friend, and they wish this friend to make their father/mother happy, and to be cordially received and not to make them feel like strangers. Although the most common situations is children being selfish in this aspect and rejection to the new person arriving to their parents' life.

To get over through the parents' divorce, children must recognize that their parents are human beings that can make mistakes, and respect them for their efforts and courage recurring to a moral and socially accepted situation. To this acceptation, children, without a doubt, must be well prepared and/or educated so those failures do not fall down on them.

Reactions presented in children before an event as painful as a breakup or a divorce, vary through different ages:

2 - 5 YEARS:

Regression, sleep disorders, irritability, anguish, need for physical contact, playfulness inhibition, fear to abandon, feelings of being responsible for the separation.

5 - 8 YEARS:

Displays of sadness, sobs, rejection feelings, longing for the missing parent, fantasies about the gone parent's return. Accentuated decrease in school performance. Fear to be expelled from their social group.

9 - 12 YEARS:

Renounce to talk about their problems, intense rage against one or both parents, decrease in school performance, social relationships deterioration, can be easily taken as an allied to one of the parents.

ADOLESCENCE:

Depression, school absenteeism, sexual activity, use of alcohol and drugs, suicidal attempts. That is why parents must be aware about their children's behavior changes, as well as the kind of friends they hang around.

Breakup or divorce is a conflict that reaches to all family members, that is why I suggest psychological support and orientation for both your children and yourself.

With the finality of reducing negative effects in your children, you must practice the next recommendations:

➢ ***Be a friend to your children and keep a close and safe communication.*** Communication is very important, truly vital.

➢ ***Both parents must reiterate they love their children very much***. Make clear to them that even though their parents are discontent with each other and have discrepancies in many things, you are in complete agreement about the love both of you maintain to your children. Show your love sharing with them.

➢ ***Keep the same environment.*** As you keep minimal the number of changes, the more manageable the crisis will be. Try to keep your children in the same house. If this is not possible, try to keep them in the same school, with the same teachers, friends and sport teams, although this can be done only temporarily.

➢ *Let them know that even their life standard may lower a little bit, their basic needs will be satisfied.* (food, clothing, place to live).

➢ *Affirm that they will see their father constantly, if this is the case.* Your children need so much their father as their mother. Divorce causes confusion in small children and makes them fear to be abandoned by one of the parents. Children need to know they will be in constant touch, as well with the father as with the mother.

➢ *Schedule visits through a defined and established plan.* The parent with the children' s custody must firmly support the visits program. A whole day every week or every two weeks is preferable than brief, more frequents but hurried visits. If there is more than a child, all of them must spend the same time quantity with the parent without custody, to avoid favoritism feelings. Your child will impatiently wait for the visits, so the visiting parent must keep its promises, being punctual and remembering birthdays and other special events. Both parents must strive to make visits pleasant.

➢ *Provide your children the phone number where the other parent can be found in order to be called regularly.* If the parent that has no custody has moved to another city, phone calls and letters become indispensables to keep a constant relationship. Explain to your children "You dad (or mom) can't visit you for now. He/she have a lot of troubles that is trying to solve. In this moment there is nothing we can do to change that situation".

➢ ***Help your children to express their frustrations and loss feelings.*** When the parents' breakup or divorce occurs, many children experience anxiety, depression and rage. Frequently, they are near to cry, do not sleep well, their stomach or head ache, and do not obtain good results at school. To help them to get through this painful feeling, encourage them to talk about them and answer them with support and understanding. A discussion group about divorce at school can help children to feel less isolated and ashamed. Your children need enough time to suffer the loss of you and your partner as united parents. Let them freely express their feelings and answer honestly to the answers they ask you. Never tell lies, otherwise they will not trust in you and sincerity is the base to a good communication.

➢ ***Express repeatedly to your children that they are not to blame for the divorce.*** Children often feel guilt, believing they somehow had something to do with divorce. Your children need to be constantly assured that they were not the cause of divorce.

➢ ***Make clear to your children that divorce is definitive.*** Some children persist in the hope of their parents being together again and they express and behave as if separation was temporal. Assume that divorce is definitive can help them to better adapt to the situation by accepting the truth.

➢ ***Protect positive opinions have about both parents.*** **It is important to remark the positive aspects of the missing father or mother. Do not express** negative feelings that **you have against you former partner (you must vent this feelings with other adult person, not with your children). Discredit or disdain the missing father or mother** before the children, can decrease children' s self-opinion and to cause more stress.

➢ ***Keep the same discipline in both homes.*** Your children need to be educated with coherent and firm rules. Exaggerated indulgence or excessive tolerance by one of the parents can make the other parent to have troubles making children to behave. Constant competition for a child's love through privileges or special gifts, gives place to a excessively spoiled children. Reasonable discipline rules must be established and both parents must respect those rules.

➢ ***Do not discuss with your former partner before your children.*** Children are very affected by seeing their parents fighting. It is very important to avoid every discussion about children' s visits, custody, support or any other issue in front of them.

➢ ***Avoid disputes over custody.*** Your children need to feel stable. Oppose to the given custody of the other parent only if it is causing any obvious harm or suffering to your children. False physical or sexual abuse accusations produce enormous emotional anguish to children. If it is possible do not separate brothers unless they are teenagers and wishing to live in different places is clearly voiced.

Therapies are of great help in most of the cases, because can provide reaffirmation and constant support to your children. Through them, a trained person other from a family member, induce children to express their discomfort and to have a better handle of their sadness, frustration, anxiety and anguish feelings.

DEEP FEELINGS THAT INVADE OUR SPIRIT

CHAOS

When separation or divorce occurs, an emotional energy is released in strong and painful feelings shape. Some will experience this kind of strong feelings as euphoria.

You feel so good that you think you are ready to face life. However those feelings do not last long.

Your euphoria is a false perception of the happenings. You are still vulnerable, sensitive and susceptible to be hurt by other persons.

As time passes euphoria decreases, because you accept that your married status has changed, you are a single person, you are not married anymore.

Most of the recently divorced persons experience a sense of loss, of immense sadness, a decay of their interior structure.

They have lost its role as a married person. There is an emotional misalignment, much confusion and a strong feeling of "non property".

Emotions tend to be overwhelming due to their intensity. You can be watching an object and without reason you begin to cry; you are speaking with your ex-spouse or with your children and without any reason you begin to shout to them. The feelings will explode if they are not controlled or canalized in a constructive way.

You are not becoming crazy nor ill, you are reacting very emotionally before a devastating experience in your life, as it is the death of a relation.

You are feeling the mourning of that death.

Take in consideration that you will heal like you heal of a wound by a fall or a slash. Eventually that hypersensitivity will become in strength and an alert status for future relations.

FEAR TO CHANGE

All the unexpected things generally produce surprise, restlessness, and in many cases fear. A fear to the unknown; on the contrary, all the well-known generates the sensation of security and stability, although we are suffering.

The main obstacle that interposes to your happiness is the fear to change. You must face it and overcome it, since the fear debilitates your physical and mental energies. It paralyzes you, stopping you to take the best decisions. The fear includes the fear to fail, to be, to rejection, etc.

The problem arises when we let ourselves get dominated by the fear and we feed it with negative thoughts. It is not easy to accept changes, because besides the fears that impede you, our form to think and to act have become something automatic. As automatic are the thoughts that maintain self-esteem low. Sometimes we do not even realize it. But if you do not overcome fear, you are not going to obtain that life that you wish.

To which we fear is to make mistakes, to not knowing how to react to an unknown situation. We have lost the capacity to see the changes like self-knowledge, growth experiences, to choose and to allow us to make mistakes. Indeed, the difference between a coward and a brave person, consist of the coward letting be taken by its fears while the brave one moves away from them and it continues his way.

There is no time to be scared, since we only lived once. In many occasions, we prayed, hopping that things happen, we believe in destiny, and we forget to act, to believe in ourselves. We get satisfied instead to take the risk, without thinking that every day that passes will never return.

Everything depends on our will, the internal force, to tell ourselves a thousand times **I can!** Your happiness depends exclusively on you, there is no one to blame, you are responsible for all your decisions. Face destiny, you only must propose it.

Remember love is that with we were born. The fear is what we have learned here. The spiritual trip is renouncing to fear and the new acceptance of love in our heart.

Each change is the possibility of being advancing in ourselves, meeting new people, to live transcendental experiences and mainly to be convinced that we are not betraying ourselves same nor to our desires.

SOLITUDE

When suffering a separation or divorce we face with the feared solitude. The fear to be lonely, paralyzes, hopelessness appears, illusions fade out and uncertainty irrupts. This solitude is painful, but it can become positive if we see it like an opportunity. Indeed, to be lonely gives back the personal power to us, offers the opportunity to analyze us, to question us, to make a balance about what we are doing is good or bad, to find us with ourselves. Besides it allows us to draw goals to new destinies that we had probably not considered.

Some people evade solitude until the point of which they prefer to be in a totally damaged relationship, or that does not make them happy, than to make the decision to finish the relation. The fear to solitude is so overwhelming that they prefer not to risk looking for another partner. Simply satisfy by telling themselves: "worse is nothing". Definitively, this one is not a good decision and demonstrates a very low self-esteem without a doubt.

Love yourself, otherwise you are not going to receive the love that you wish ever. Trust in the wonderful person that you are.

Get rid of your mind and let go all those thoughts that make you feel victim of the circumstances. Remember "You decide", "You choose" what kind of life you wish.

You deserve to be happy...

Remember that suffering because of love is not necessary. Love is happiness, to feel well, it cheers, and gives us harmony.

If you are in a relation and you do not receive the love that you wish, you must begin to look for a solution, but not in the other, but within you. Your pair reflects your internal state, not handled by you of conscious form. We think that the other is guilty, and hide the true problem, that it is the low self-esteem, you do not give the love and respect that yourself is requiring, which makes impossible that another person can give it to you. Solution is in your hands. Love, respect and love yourself.

It is very common to listen that one of the main causes of the unhappiness or misfortune is solitude and although it does not constitute an upheaval in itself, normally is associated to frustration and displeasure feelings, that frequently end at situations that lead to depression. Now, the solitude can become a great ally to obtain and to enjoy success. Everything depends on you.

Only when we are single we can get in touch with ourselves. That opportunity allows us to evaluate if we really are like we want to be and if we are doing what we wished to do; and if that image were not in agreement with our expectations, it is the moment for asking to us, what are we doing to obtain it.

DEPRESSION

Affliction is the answer to the pain that arises when losing somebody important for you. Immediately after a separation, divorce or loss, you can feel insensible and empty, as if you were in shock state and you will be able to notice physical changes, like tremors, nausea, problems to breathe, muscular weakness, dry mouth or problems to sleep and to eat. You can have nightmares, being distracted, moved away from society, or not having desire to return to work or to fulfill your activities and daily obligations.

Duration of affliction depends on the time that takes you to accept the loss and to learn to live with it; it is different in each person, to some lasts only months and to others, years. Many reasons for these differences exist, including the cultural aspect, personality, health, familiar background referring to the handling of emotions, the quality of the relation and the experiences of life.

Each person who undergoes a separation, divorce, or loss, must complete its process accepting the experience, tolerating and feeling the physical and emotional pain of the loss, adapting to live without the pair. This way, the person will be able to close that chapter of its life and to begin again.

Depression is an emotional disorder that can be transitory or permanent, it is able to affect clinically not only the mind but the body, requiring in many cases being treated clinically. It has a multi-factor origin, being sentimental deception one of the triggering factors. The most frequent symptoms are: a sensation of sadness and almost permanent pessimism, anxious mood; loss of interest or pleasure in the activities that the person used to enjoy; low energy, fatigue, feeling of "slowness; " changes in the sleep patterns; loss or increase of appetite; loss or gain of weight; problems to concentrate, to remember and to make decisions; guilt and negativity feelings; uselessness or neglect; death referred thoughts or suicide; recurring malaise and pains that do not respond to treatment.

If the symptoms before indicated persist and your spirit do not improve, you must look for qualified help.

DENIAL

One of the first reactions that separated or divorced person must confront is denial, which is a normal reaction. In some cases, the person repeats frequently:

"This is not really happening to me, I will awake and everything will have been a bad dream"

Denial can get to be really worrisome, when it is not surpassed in a brief period of time.

In order to overcome this situation, it is recommendable that you repeat yourself and to others "I am separated or I am divorced", according to the case, and later mentally close smoothly the door of your relation or marriage.

Also it is advisable to internally recognize that your relation or marriage failed for many reasons, but that in no case this is translated in the fact that you are a failure like person.

It accepts the reality so that you can open yourself to a new life. Close that chapter of your life as rapidly as possible, do not hook you in the past, a shining future awaits for you.

RAGE OR WRATH

A huge number of emotions that could be undergone during the separation process or divorce exist, among them the rage or wrath, which is a sudden reaction of aggressive violent type. The rage access produces vegetative-nervous that can be pronounced in the form of sweat, pallor or on the contrary out of proportion reddening of the face, tremors, gestures with shouts and violence, passionate feelings of hatred that diminish the reason. These emotions' noxious effects harm so much familiar, social as well as labor life.

Some people hide their wrath in the deepest of their being, which can physically manifest through headaches, stomach or any other type of malaise. Perhaps simply you feel bad with yourself and begin to cry. It is no healthy to hide wrath, it is necessary to release it without hurting anybody, including you.

The rage is only one of the emotions that the separated or divorced person, in many cases, must confront during this period of crisis. These feelings or emotions will disappear when you accept the outcome and you confront that moment of transition. Whether you have given the welcome to the divorce, or that you have been dragged to it, kicking and screaming, you have lost something of great importance.

Mourning is a process that has its own natural rhythm, but we can use this time to process our feelings, identifying them, sharing them and expressing them in a positive and constructive way, obtaining pain to become less intense and more bearable.

Do not lose control. To get even with others does not solve anything. However, to recognize that you are angry and trying to know why and how to avoid that situation to be repeated, makes the difference.

It is advisable to speak about your rage, since when you express it with words, those negative feelings usually begin to disappear. Nevertheless, we cannot become self-destructive, reason why I recommend to you to put in practice the following:

> **Identify** your wrath's source, your irrational thoughts that make you understand as unfair some situations

> **Relax**, count until 10, breathe deep and slowly and repeat yourself "calm down, everything is alright", "reassure yourself".

➢ **Receive** or give a hug as a sign of love and protection.

➢ Repeat positive statements as, "I must take things easy", "calm down", "everything is alright"

➢ **Learn** to express calmly, develop an assertive behavior

➢ **Accept** people as they are and avoid to constantly judge people

➢ **Do not do** alcohol or drugs, that only will make worse the problem

➢ **Practice** some kind of play or sport, sing, dance, draw your anger

➢ **Do not let rage to take control over you, take control of your life for your own well-being.**

"You can, trust in you"

GUILT

Guilt is the emotion that squanders major amount of emotional energy, it immobilizes you in the present for a past event. It is not a natural way to behave, it is a learned emotional reaction and it has different degrees, from a small inconvenience to a severe depression. One of its more common consequences is remorse, that it is defined as the internal grief that it is produced in the soul due to have done a bad action.

It is easy to blame others and not assuming the responsibility of what happened. To blame somebody else is one of the safest ways to follow with a problem. When blaming others we renounce to our power. The soonest you recognize this truth, the faster you will begin the path to recovery. We must honestly face who we are and how we are related to others. In another way, it is very likely that errors committed in your relation or marriage will repeat and affect your future relations.

This new moment in your life, in which you are "single or unmarried" it is an ideal opportunity for analyzing yourself and to review your values and you norms of life, to recognize your errors and to work on yourself. Begin to watch the past like something impossible to modify, you feel what you feel respect to it "it is over", and your guilt feeling will not change it.

Focus in your self-esteem, you must love, value, respect and accept yourself just as you are. Ask yourself about the realities and opportunities that you are evading in the present because of the past, working in this aspect you will eliminate your guilt necessity.

STRESS

When a relation finishes, there is a loss or change of structure in the life of people, which produces a very great stress and that is translated in significant changes in your daily habits, as they are it:

On the other hand, we can see that some people deal to obstruct your decision to leave a relation that makes you suffer and in other occasions they seemed to push you to keep it; then, when what happens is that the relation is finished, they label to you as a failed person and they deal to you with pity.

Social pressure always is going to be present. All want to give their opinions on the basis of their own experiences, sometimes and some persons do it with bad faith and others with good faith. For that reason I suggest you to forget about society and to guide your steps directly to which truly makes you happy. Look for the answers inside of you and listen to people who really loves you.

Do not let themconfuse you, nor make you feel like a failed person, all the answers are in your interior. To construct an unshakeable self-esteem and a high concept of your-self is the definitive cure to overcome social pressure or fear to rejection.

CONFUSION

After a separation, the confusion is very frequent, for that reason you must examine some concrete points of it and act. You must take firm control of your life. Decide to take a step every day. Firstly you must change the negative mental habit of despising your-self. People, generally, do not recognize that they have this habit. When you despise yourself, you are counting failures. This conduct can be neutralized if you put your attention in the positive things made by you every day regardless how small they are. In order to make of this exercise a habit, you must make it every day for at least five weeks.

FORGIVENESS

Forgiveness is the experience of peace and understanding that feels in the present. It is a love expression. Forgiveness makes us free from knots that poison our soul and sicken our body. Lack of forgiveness ties you to people from the base of resentment. Forgiveness is the master key to happiness, is a gift for yourself, it is to give yourself peace.

Forgiveness is not other thing than load shedding of the sentimental weights that torment us and that prevent us from continuing our path towards well-being. We must forgive for our own sake, since feelings of rage, wrath or pain that we lived when we do not forgive, affect spiritual and physically to us, besides driving us into a negative spiral that poisons our soul.

To ask for forgiveness is the same than apologize. When apologizing you are expressing that you are really feeling the damage that you have done, even though you have not done it consciously. When you apologize and you do it sincerely, it means that you have paused to think about the feeling that you caused into the victimized person. After apologizing, surely you will feel better and that also will happen to the other person.

There are many ways to apologize, like for example: " I feel very for telling you those displeasing words", "I lost the stirrups, I did not should have insulted you, I am sorry" , " I am sorry for hurting your feelings" , "it will not happen again." When you apologize, it is possible that person also offer apologies to you. Nevertheless, the important thing is the action to apologize, that means recognition of the committed error and the intention of not repeating it.

In case that your ex- pair apologizes to you, it is possible that you do not feel immediately desire to return to a friendship, that takes time. Also it can happen that if your pair has behaved badly to you repeatedly, it does not change. On the other hand, you could feel a lightening when listening apologies and cheer you due to the recognition by the other person of it own mistakes. In any case, the fact that a person apologizes does not mean that you are automatically forced to integrate it to your life again. That is something that is only up to you.

To forgive does not mean to deny the happened painful facts, on the contrary is the powerful affirmation with which those negative facts will not ruin your present, even though it have affected your past that is why I recommend you not constructing a resentment history that only drives you internal destruction.

Indeed, forgiveness does not produce amnesia, it is not totally indispensable that we forget to pardon, since I can forgive and be conscious of the damage that was done to me, but I decide it is no longer going to affect me. The pardon is a mechanism to heal our heart wounds.

The pardon is a mechanism to heal our heart wounds. Without forgiveness there is no peace. If you want to maintain a healthy balance within your-self and want to advance in the spiritual and healing path, you must pardon with the heart and forget. It is as important to forgive as to forget because often without forgetfulness there is no forgiveness. There are those who usually say "I do forgive, but do not forget" and with that philosophy it is demonstrated that the resentment keeps on validity, without realizing that resentment is a poison that lies in the soul, but that also sickens the body.

Do not give anybody the power to make you unhappy. Forgive because you decide to do it, take again your immense capacity to construct your own calm.

It is necessary to forgive from heart, not only to others but to ourselves and that is even more difficult. It is definitely, the best thing than we can do by our own sake, so that we can be able to continue our free path without unnecessary loads that become immense obstacles to obtain our happiness.

CAUSE AND EFFECT IN YOUR LIFE

 When you have already passed and lived forgiveness you understand by your own experience the so called Law of Cause and Effect which is a life law that many people do not take into account, and that is really the most important to be able to obtain good results in all the aspects of our life.

This is a law also know as Law of Consequence, Repayment or Compensation. A law that works perfectly in all aspects and brings to accomplishment everything what we seeded, in thought, word and action. This means that everything that you do puts in movement a cause and this one brings a consequence, positive or negative, that will depend on the cause placed in movement. Chance, good luck or bad luck, does not exist, only results. This law tells us that there are certain causes for success and determined causes for failure; that there are specific causes for health and disease and that also there is for happiness and unhappiness.

In your daily life you have responsibilities to fulfill what you do not have to evade, if you evade you will have to make the pertinent corrections and the more you evade them, the correction that you must do it will be more difficult and laborious, because consequences are irreversible. Even your "apparently insignificant" acts can affect many people and of those consequences we will be directly responsible, and the own law will demand its payment, that is not another thing that the process to learn to build well with love, sincerity and honesty.

As you are evolutionary and imperfect being you are exposed to commit errors. An honestly committed mistake, with sincere intention to be constructive, will have to be corrected by all means, but the correction will be more severe if you try to evade your own responsibilities or do deliberately what you know that is harmful only to satisfy your personal desires.

Before the crisis of a separation, this simple law in which you have to focus leaves perplex the majority of people. The people, by system, time and again make or repeat those things or situations that produce unhappiness and frustration to them, blaming others and society fortheir problems. Even is commented that it is folly to do the same things in the same way with the hope to obtain different results.

In a certain way you as well as I have fallen in this in more than an occasion. What you must do is to openly confront to this tendency and to try to correct it.

To show you the simple mechanism of the Law of Cause and Effect, I say to you that if you usually have negative feelings like envy, greed, or resentment and you usually think negatively referring to your life and the one of the other people, mainly the one of your ex- pair, the results are then negatives towards your person. And if on the contrary you think positive and fight so that every day you get better, then you will get positive results. If you change the quality of your thoughts, you will change the quality of your life.

The change of your outer experience will bring with itself the change of your inner experience. You will gather what you have seeded as negative or positive. Your thought is the weapon most important to achieve your objectives. If you wish good things to other, then you will be at the same time wishing good things to yourself.

Never forget this law in your separation process since your attitudes, words and thoughts are going to repel in your future ether near or distant. Nobody can evade the action of this law.

Once you create the cause, you will not be able to flee from the consequence regardless how astute you are. The consequence will come infallibly more early or later. If it does not come from some form, it will come from another form.

Then, what you have to do always is, to create good thoughts, good words and good actions in your daily life, in order that you form good habits and moral convention; this will allow you to cultivate a good character and a good personality to create a full destiny of happiness.

The principle "things alike attract things alike", means that the thoughts that a person maintains in its mind (conscious or unconscious), the emotions, beliefs and actions attract consequences which they correspond to positive or negative experiences, that is to say, your thoughts determine your experience. We are the creators of our destiny.

In this order of ideas, the creative process contemplates three steps, that is to say:

FIRST STEP: TO ASK

You must ask for what you wish, you do not need to use words. The universe will respond to your thoughts, feelings and emotions. Take this step faithfully.

SECOND STEP: ANSWER TO YOUR WISHES

This is not your task in a physical manner, the universe will do it for you. The universe will start to restructure so that what you really wish will manifest. You do not know how, but you will attract the way, persons, coincidences and circumstances.

THIRD STEP: RECEIVING

You must be in accordance with which you want. To be enthusiastic, to be glad, to do what you must do to generate the feelings to have it now, this will help you to attract it. For example, try to drive test the automobile of your dreams or visit the house that you wish. Be thankful as if you already had received your order and most important feel as if you have already obtained it.

Human beings generally, repeat their patterns of conduct, even though you do not feel satisfied with the obtained results. If you do not feel satisfied with your life, learn from your mistakes and modify your habits, surely you will obtain new results; but if you keep the same pattern, without a doubt you will continue obtaining the same undesired results.

It is not easy to stop our negative thoughts, and to avoid that they settle in our lives, for it we must focus in seeding every day a greater number of positive thoughts. Also, I suggest to you that when negativity assaults you, you use some of these tools: be thankful for being alive and all the good things that you have and surround to you, listen to music that produces joy to you, do some activity that pleases you, visualize fulfilling your goals, repeat your favorite positive affirmations, do exercise, meditation or yoga.

Finally, you must choose the tools that work better for you to feel well and not allow that negativity seizes you.

By virtue of all the exposed, I recommend to you to seed positive thoughts deliberately, to choose always "to feel well", regardless of which it happens to you, to keep watching your emotional guidance independent from what happens to you, that is to say, that your beliefs and emotions stay in the scope of the love, peace and harmony, joy, tranquility, tolerance, compassion and gratefulness. Focus exclusively in everything that you wish, in thought, feeling, word and action and surely you will prevail. We are 100% in charge to create our lives.

The universe will work accurately to obey this Law. What you see in front of you is the exact manifestation of your thoughts.

Finally, for your knowledge, I enumerate other Universal principles or Laws as important as the Law of Cause and Effect or Law of Attraction, before commented:

¬ Law of Mentalism: "The whole is mind; the universe is mental".

¬ Law of Correspondence: "As it is above, it is down; as it is down, it is above".

¬ Law of Vibration: "Nothing rests; everything moves; everything vibrates".

¬ Law of Polarity: "Everything is dual; everything has its pair of opposite; like and unlike are the same; opposed are identical in nature, but different in degree; all the truths are not but half truths; all the paradoxes can be reconciled".

¬ Law of Rhythm: Everything flows, outside and inside; everything has its tides; all the things raise and fall; the oscillation of the pendulum is pronounced in everything; the measurement of oscillation towards the right is the measurement of the oscillation towards the left; the rate compensates".

¬ Law of Gender: Gender is in everything; everything has its masculine and feminine principles; the sort is pronounced in every plane.

TO ACCEPT AND LET GO LOVE AGAIN

Acceptance is absolutely necessary for you evolution. "To accept and let go" it is like freeing oneself from the past, to begin life like present, beginning to accept us as we are, including the imperfections.

It is to stop fighting with life, to accept people as they are, as well as situations, circumstances and events that appear to you, including decisions and actions of the past, good as much as bad.

Not to blame anybody not even ourselves for the negative situations in which sometimes we have been immersed.

You think you love to those who surround you, but, sometimes they become incomprehensible for you, like you become incomprehensible for them.

Everything that exists in the physical plane, including people, is in constant transformation, sometimes this disturbs you and even it distresses you, but that is called to evolve.

You must accept this transformation in yourself you and others.

You must accept the challenges and the suffering that makes you be born again. Nevertheless, you are free to advance at your own pace, according to what you think of you and others.

If you do not let yourself be beaten by your ego, surely you will obtain the knowledge necessary to advance to a new challenge in your life. First of all, it resigns to grasp to what is not for you, and in some circumstances, impossible to obtain, "To accept and To let go", will allow you to live in the present tense, open totally to all the possibilities that the life offers to you, without grasping rigidly to none of them.

Not everything is under your control or dominion and sometimes is difficult to know when is advisable to continue fighting or when is advisabl "To accept and let go". Besides analyzing the situation in an objective way, it is necessary that you request aid to your supreme being, GOD. In this point it seems pertinent to me to mention serenity prayer:

"Lord, concede me serenity
TO ACCEPT the things that I cannot change,
COURAGE to change those that I can and
WISDOM to recognize the difference"

Close your eyes, render up to your supreme being and let it act, close the eyes of the soul and say calmly "Jesus I trust you" and you will see great miracles.

CLOSING OF THE PAST OPENS A NEW DAWN

So that you can open to a new dawn you must begin to close that cycle that finished.

You must forget and bury your bad experience, learn from your errors and follow way.

This process can be long and stormy or can be short and stimulating, according to what you decide. The results that you obtain are going to repel not only in you, but also in your children, parents and brothers, and aim in your familiar surroundings.

If you feel cornered or trapped and you do not know what to do to change or to improve your situation, ask for help.

I suggest a relative, friend or a therapist for you, must be a person who really has the capacity, knowledge and objectivity for helping to find the best solution.

If you are working in your self-esteem, you will more likely need the aid of someone that has experienced this aspect. Whenever you are discouraged and you want to return to your previous conduct, it recalls to mind and it thinks that although it is painful or difficult at those moments, you are constructing the bases for a better life, reason why you cannot return back.

An excellent therapy is to write in a paper everything what it saddens, disturbs or worries you and then, without reading it, you tear it or burn it, do it whichever times is necessary. Also you can record it and erase it without hearing it, because if you listen to it, it will not give the same result to you and it will not be an effective short term therapy.

Always keep in mind the image that you are going to obtain and how you are going to feel. Visualize your profits, feeling them, living them. Why to imagine the worse? if you can imagine the best thing.

Do not be trapped by fear. Remember that you are the owner of your thoughts.

You generate them and you can change them by others and when we changed our way to think, they change our feelings, conducts and our life generously.

Choose to open a new page in the book of your existence, closing the chapter of the past in your life.

The important thing is to be able to get free of the moments of your life that have closed. The relation has finished? It is over, understand it from the deepest of your heart, because if not, you will spend long time of your present, trying to understand what happened.

If you persist in that feeling, the wearing down is going to be infinite, going to be a labyrinth without exit.

When you finish with stages or moments of life, you have to watch and to follow forward. You cannot be in the present longing for the past. Not even asking you why. It is necessary to go on.

We cannot continue having a bond with those who do not want to be linked to us.

Because you deserve the best, being happy.

"TO LOVE AND TO BE LOVED"

Do not let the past to prevent you from advancing, continue your way. Forgive and forget and do not give place to resentment.

Dedicate yourself to review the matter, the reasons or causes that happened, the all you will get is to be mentally hurt and embitter yourself without no necessity.

Life is going ahead, never going back, because if you go around life leaving open chapters, you will never be able to get free of the things that happened, nor to live the present with satisfaction.

Close the past for your mental health, for your pride, and free yourself from what is no longer there in your life, keep going ahead, draw up your new way, make it step by step, with delivery, faith, optimism and mainly with love.

THE GREAT GOODBYE AND YOUR NEW SELF

The encounter with yourself, is one of the signals of greater importance in order to show you that you already have said goodbye to the chapter of sadness, frustration and anger which you suffered by the loss of the loved person and you are initiating the process of welcome to your new self.

Between the signals that commonly are observed during this new process, the following are important:

- The anger towards the ex- pair or ex- spouse stops being an obsession 24 hours a day and it is diminishing day by day, until arriving at non frequent sparkles of wrath.

- You spend less time in complaining about problems and more time in solving them.

- You begin to contact again with your true friends.

- You open yourself to new friendships.

- You stop getting embarrassed.

- You accept the separation or divorce as the unique possible solution to a destructive marriage and no longer you see it as a punishment or failure.

- You begin to discover your own tastes and your own interests again.

- You no longer label opposite sex, like threatening or despicable.

- You realize that you are not the unique person who has divorced, and that other people have had the anger to finish an unfortunate marriage.

In this stage you are playing a new roll, the one of a new person, whom has forgiven others and oneself, leaving back resentment. Someone who has decided to be happy.

Go on, the success is yours!

GET THE NEW LOVE THAT IS WAITING FOR YOU

Everything in life implies action, consciousness, this is the reason why I recommend you to use some strategies, to attract it:

PREPARE AS MUCH IN THE MENTAL ASPECT, AS IN THE PHYSICAL ASPECT.

In the mental aspect, feel sure of yourself, deserving the love that you wish, open to receive it. Decree it. Set a date. Visualize it. It will help you to write a list of all the aspects that you would like that your ideal pair had. Cover with detail the characteristics about which you dream, from the physical aspect to the spiritual affinity. Be the most specific as possible and soon it will recreate that image in your mind the greater amount of time as possible.

In the physical, change or modify the decoration of your house, give, dull or sell all those objects that bring bad memories to you. Regarding your physical aspect, take care of your feeding, do exercise, and any other change that makes you feel better, for example: change the color of your hair, or make a different haircut.

RECOMMENDED ACTIONS

- Begin to make new friendships and to contact the old ones.

- Register in some course of your interest, attend events, do not reject invitations, visit new places and change your routine.

- Frequent places in agreement with the type of person that you look for, for example: if you have preference by the sportsmen attends sport events, register in a gymnasium. If you like intellectuals subscribe into a course or studio, be part of a circle of readers, attend cultural events. If you like plastic arts lovers, visit galleries of art or exhibitions.

- Let know to your friendships, that you are open to meet new people and that you are available to accept new invitations, aiming that they present his friends or fellow workers to you.

- Give yourself a chance to open to love, give it your welcome, focus your thoughts towards the profit of that goal and you will surely attract it.

A RELATIONSHIP IS ALWAYS FOR BEING BETTER

A good relation is a commitment between two, where both must be loved, respected, helped and mutually accepted as they are. Nobody is perfect; in fact, perfect affective relations do not exist.

Life is easy to take peacefully, harmony and happiness, but human beings have their fears and prejudices, that make them difficult and complicated. In no case, a relation is for competing, changing the other or to unload the neuroses that we suffer.

Definitively, the relationship supposes a conscious commitment of the parts to share their lives to feel better.

You don't suffer because of love.

You don't suffer for being happy.

If you are in a relation and they do not love you as you wish, you suffer or you do not feel satisfied, you must begin to look for a solution, not in others but in you. The answers always are in ourselves, but sometimes we get blinded before situations that we do not want to face.

Sometimes we ask the other person to change, so that we think that it is the culprit of our misfortune and the problem we have is really ourselves and is transformed in low self-esteem, you do not give yourself the value you deserve. In this case, you must work hard on yourself and remember whenever a relationship is always for being better.

ATTRACT A GOOD LOVE BEING YOU

Get open to receive the love that you deserve simply being you. You do not require to copy anybody or to acquire poses.

You must behave at any moment being the person that you are. You are astonishing, unique and unrepeatable. Strive in being satisfied with yourself, instead of forcing in pleasing others by pretending.

A relation begins long before than when you found your pair, begins when you find yourself. You must be ready emotionally so that the relation is successful and you do not repeat old patterns. In addition it turns out useful to make external changes in your physical aspect as in your home.

Do not feel alone or sad, the person that you are waiting for exists, you only must open your mind and soul to attract it.

YOUR NEW LOVE AND YOUR CHILDREN

When divorce has already been completed, new problems for children arise. One of them is originated when you resume your social life or you begin a new relation, your children feel that you are allowing the entrance of strange people to the house, so that they occupy the place of the absent parent, consequently will feel resentment in some cases. Your children will perceive these people as a replacement of the absent parent and in many cases feel a deep resentment.

When appointments become habitual, children tend to act with revolt, disobeying orders that commonly fulfilled for obligation so you pay more attention to them, intensifying the jealousy.

A qualified guide will allow you to construct a successful future for you and it will turn you into an assertive person able to confront your challenges, superimposing any obstacle that appears in your way; you will be able to handle your thoughts, feelings and emotions in a balanced way orienting them towards the profit of your objectives; to release the emotional pain, to eliminate the patterns of self-destructive thoughts, among other aspects.

Nothing is impossible, all you must do is make the decision and choose to take action, we offer our services to you through the Webpage www.tuestima.com, you would find there the tools that you need to secure the emotional state that you really wish. A relation, remember, is always for being better and you deserve to love and to be loved.

TO BE BORN AGAIN

Now that you are a new person, balanced, who loves itself, that is approved and respected, and has controlled its emotions; I propose to you a series of strategies with the purpose to complete this wonderful process that you confronted with bravery, faith, and perseverance. Congratulations…

Make a life project in which you shape your dreams and your yearnings. Plan objectives to short, medium and long term, since they are the bases to construct your project of life.

Establish a departure point for each objective that is according with your reality, taking care of your conditions and possibilities.

Identify the actions to follow to fulfill each objective.

Do a list of your qualities or strengths and your weaknesses, aiming to explain the actions to work on these last ones and to manage to optimize the results.

Review your conduct before important events in the past, with the unique intention to take positive aspects.

Aiming to give fulfillment to that indicated before, you will have to put in practice the following:

Decree the fulfillment of your desires. Visualize them.

Always keep the security that you will be able to solve the adverse situations that appear to you.

You do not give up and never ignore friends opinions directed to the fulfillment of your objectives.

Always keep a high level of your self-esteem to be able to obtain what you set out.

START YOUR NEW DAY

Aiming to accompany you in this wonderful process, we offer you a variety to positive affirmations and a series of phrases that stimulate your power, both will contribute with your well-being.

On this page we especially created for you, copy and paste it in a place where it you can read every day aloud, and to repeat and firmness frequently.

POSITIVE AFFIRMATIONS:

The beginning of the affirmations consists of choosing the own thoughts and repeatedly using them the number of times that is necessary so that your creative force produces results in the real world. Use the affirmations applicable to your life and your present moment.

I, (your name)…., Now……

1. I love myself and I am approved as I am.

2. I am free of being myself.

3. I let love arrive in my life and fill me with happiness and joy.

4. I express my own beauty in everything I do.

5. I open my heart and accept others as they are.

6. I accept the pleasure like part of myself.

7. I listen to my feelings and express them in an appropriate form.

8. I radiate peace, calm and optimism.

9. I open my imagination to create the best of the worlds for me.

10. I feel my internal harmony.

11. I am loved and I am love.

12. I am perfect as I am. Everything in my life happens for my good.

13. I am a loved creature of the universe.

14. I trust myself, I trust my intuition, I am peaceful.

15. I am the perfect synchronism in my life, my world and all subjects.

16. I am forgiven as I forgive those who have hurt me.

17. I open myself to a new life filled with happiness.

18. I love myself no matter what happens.

19. My life is wonderful.

20. I have the best family in the world.

21. I am a magnet to attract the perfect couple.

22. I have all my paths opened.

23. I deserve funny, healthy and sincere relationships.

24. I deserve to be happy.

25. I deserve the best of life.

26. I deserve the perfect work

27. My perfect pair has already arrived to my life.

28. All desires become reality.

29. I do love and I am loved.

30. I am abundance.

31. I am health.

32. The money arrives to me easily and fluidly.

33. As of today, the luck wraps to me completely.

34. Today I let myself receive the abundance of life.

35. I open myself to receive what by divine law corresponds to me.

36. I feel out of danger and protected.

37. All the ways are open for me.

38. There is no negative energy that affects me.

39. I have the power and the blessing to receive the ideas of God, the divine abundance and the divine prosperity.

40. All the things that I desire for my family and myself have arrived here and now in a perfect and harmonic way for everybody.

41. I love life, I love Love itself.

42. The prosperity is in me.

43. Money arrives to me without effort.

44. I feel peacefully, because I am conscious of the guide and protection of God

45. I feel peacefully with coming back to consciousness.

46. Here and now all my desires are fulfilled.

47. I have faith in life. I have faith in me.

48. Today I have the certainty that everything that happens to me is for my own sake.

49. Holy Spirit guide me, I know that everything that I desire for my family and myself is coming and arriving here and now. Thanks Father who already have listened to me.

50. I have the certainty that today is a wonderful day for me.

51. I can do it, I will do it, and I do it.

52. I respect the beliefs of the others.

53. I accept my internal limitations.

PHRASES (WRITTEN BY AUTHORS SEVERAL)

1. You can. Trust yourself. The power is within you. Live to fullness.

2. Dare to create the type of life that you yearn with high confidence in yourself.

3. A pair relationship is always for being better.

4. Be open to love, welcome it and you will surely attract it.

5. Each new dawn brings new blessings and miracles. Be thankful.

6. Do not grant anybody the power to make you unhappy.

7. You must dare to defy the limits that can sabotage your success NOBODY'S WORTH MORE THAN YOU!

8. When we really want something, there is no obstacle able to interpose.

9. Everything that arrives in your life you are attracting it by virtue of the images that you maintain in your mind, that you think and express verbally.

10. Your thoughts determine your experiences. We are creators of our destiny.

11. Sowing positive thoughts and negatives thoughts will be lowered.

12. We are 100% people in charge to create our lives.

13. What you see in front of you, is the exact manifestation of your thoughts.

14. There is no time to be scared. We only live once.

15. Always choose to be happy.

16. Eliminate once and for all the habits that still tie you and prevent you to reach what you truly want in your life.

17. Get connected with your own greatness and begin to live with passion and enthusiasm. Do it, you can.

18. Learn to love yourself with your defects and virtues.

19. The spiritual trip is the resignation of fear and the acceptance of love in our heart.

20. Think great, act great and you will get greatness, creating miracles in your life.

21. Forgiveness is the masterful key for happiness. It is a gift to yourself. It is to give yourself Peace.

22. Accept the fact that you are in the place and time in which you must be.

23. Live in the present tense, here and now. It is the unique moment which we have.

24. The past has fled, what you are waiting for is absent, but the present is yours.

25. Regardless how long the storm is, the sun always returns between the clouds.

26. Happiness is not to do what one wants, but to want what one does.

27. Never stop dreaming, only try to see the signals that take you to it.

28. When you really desire something, the whole universe conspires for helping you to obtain it.

29. Every day God gives us a little moment in which it is possible to change what makes us unhappy. The magical moment is when a yes or a no cannot change our existence.

Denisse Troconis Aoun & Mara Salas

POWERFUL PRAY

We allowed ourselves to transcribe a really wonderful oration very textually, to consider that it can be very useful for you.

Make of me an instrument of Peace.

That where is hatred, I bring Love.
That where is offense, I bring Forgiveness.
That where is discord, I bring Union.
That where is doubt, I bring Faith.
That where is error, I bring the Truth.
That where is desperation, I bring Hope.
That where is sadness, I bring Joy.
That where is dark, I bring Light.
That I do not look for to be consoled, but to console;
That I do not look for to be understood, but to understand;
That I do not look for to be loved, but to love.
Because giving it is as we receive,
Forgiving is as we has been forgiven,
And forgetting it is as is the eternal happiness is found.

OUR PURPOSE FOR YOU

This book has been written with much love, faith and hope, with the sincere and honest intention of bringing you the necessary tools so that you find again yourself, from love. You are an unique and wonderful being, filled with opportunities, deserving happiness, for that reason:

NOBODY'S WORTH MORE THAN YOU

You have to focus in seeing the changes in your life as self-knowledge, growth experiences, to choose and mainly of an infinite freedom, the freedom to allow you to make mistakes and to change time and again. We hope with all our heart that our effort contributes with your personal improvement, and we offer our support to you through the Webpage www.tuestima.com, that accompanies you in your wonderful path towards well-being, Peace, harmony happiness.

ABOUT THE AUTHORS

DENISSE TROCONIS AOUN:

"Like all the important things that usually happen in our lives, Mara Rooms and I met by coincidence; fact in which without a doubt the providence took part. I worked in a hotel company of prestige in the United States, and Mara wrote articles for the company, from its own company.

Any other day, we began to work together, and to interchange opinions and thus, as the sea and river encounter and rest in the same border, we entered a conversation on our personal life, and it immediately observes a reporting line between the problem and the solution.

In this case, I was the problem and Mara was my solution. I was crossing by one serious situation, no longer knew where I was going, or if I were changing of life or of year, if I were separating or living a divorce, the case is the same, I was absolutely lost. My life then was a labyrinth and I did not know what to make with it, then Mara was the light in my way, that provided the suitable and opportune answers to me to the questions that were appearing to me, most significant for myself, did help myself to believe again in me.

Mara besides being a writer is a psychologist graduated in the University of Illinois in Chicago, USA. She concentrates herself more than in being coaching psychologist and has more than 30 years of experience, with training in life coaching in New York with Holistic Learning Center Academy, Inc.".

MARA SALAS:

"To have met Denisse Troconis Aoun, especially in those circumstances, was a very special experience because my first contact with her was not like client but like a fellow worker. Having a discussion with her of inherent activities to work and general life, I reached the conclusion that she needed my aid urgently, which made me comment that I also dedicated myself to help people to solve their problems of any nature, guiding them with a therapy called life coaching.

Honestly, that is which makes me happy, I like people, and I feel that I have the ability to provide people the strength and power that they need so its self-esteem grows and believe in themselves. Denisse was living through a very difficult stage in which its logic, did not have sense, in spite of being a person very prepared professionally, was not it for the process that was living.

Fortunately, my supreme being gave me the ability of being able to orient her and to remove her from her labyrinth, seemed to me unacceptable that such a special person as she is, was living through that situation. I feel very proud to have contributed with her to appear again. In addition I did not only earned a great friend, but the immense satisfaction to see her happy, stable and retaking her way.

As a result of this event that I describe like a blessing, the idea arose to write this guide or manual, to help elevate the self-esteem of all those that have undergone a separation that has hit its lives at any level.

Denisse since very young has an inclination for the world of metaphysics, for that reason she decided to make the necessary studies to credit hersef like Life Coach, his experience in sales, trade and their knowledge of businesses acquired in the MBA, made her feel apt to conduct a battle to help people to be happy.

We unite our experiences and we focused in writing the present book "Recovering You Happiness" and we as well began our innovating project online based on website that provides aid and support to you when you need www.tuestima.com"